Down Syndrome

BY MICHELLE LEVINE

amicus
high interest

CHILDREN'S LIBRARY

Amicus High Interest is an imprint of Amicus
P.O. Box 1329, Mankato, MN 56002
www.amicuspublishing.us

Library of Congress Cataloging-in-Publication Data
Levine, Michelle, author.
 Down syndrome / by Michelle Levine.
    pages cm. — (Living with—)
 Summary: "Describes what it is like to live with Down
syndrome, what its symptoms are, and how it is treated"—
Provided by publisher.
 Audience: K to grade 3.
 Includes bibliographical references and index.
 ISBN 978-1-60753-481-5 (library binding) —
 ISBN 978-1-60753-694-9 (ebook)
1. Down syndrome—Juvenile literature. 2. Down syndrome—
Treatment—Juvenile literature. I. Title. II. Title: Down syndrome.
 RJ506.D68L48 2015
 616.85'8842—dc23

                                    2013034223

Editors   Kristina Ericksen and Rebecca Glaser
Series Designer   Kathleen Petelinsek
Designer Heather Dreisbach
Photo Researcher   Kurtis Kinneman

Photo Credits: Denis Kuvaev/Shutterstock, cover; Phanie/
SuperStock, 5; Ricki Rosen/CORBIS SABA, 7; Phanie/
SuperStock, 8; Markus Moellenberg/Corbis, 11; Bubbles
Photolibrary/Alamy, 12; Tips Images/SuperStock, 15; Jeff
Greenberg/age fotostock/SuperStock, 16; Reproduced
by permission of the Langdon Down Museum of Learning
Disability www.langdondownmuseum.org.uk, 19; Phanie/
SuperStock, 20; Belinda Images/SuperStock, 23; Washington
Post/Getty Images, 24; karelnoppe/Shutterstock, 27; BL/BSIP/
SuperStock, 28

Printed in the United States of America at Corporate Graphics
in North Mankato, Minnesota.

10 9 8 7 6 5 4 3 2

Table of Contents

What Is Down Syndrome?

This boy has **Down syndrome**. Learning new things is hard for him. So is speaking clearly. Some movements are also hard. His body does not always move how he wants it to. Sometimes he needs extra help from parents and teachers. But he is a good friend. And he loves to have fun.

This boy likes to play games.
But he might need some help.

Down syndrome affects the brain and body. That makes some things harder to do. One big thing is learning. Reading, math, and writing are harder. Many people with Down syndrome do learn these skills. It just takes longer.

Kids with Down syndrome work hard to learn new things.

This girl takes a special class.
It helps with her speech.

 My friend has Down syndrome. Why is her speech hard to understand?

Most people with Down syndrome are born with weak muscles. That makes some movements difficult. Babies learn to crawl and walk later. Some kids have trouble using buttons and zippers. Using forks or spoons may be hard, too. The muscles get stronger as the kids grow up. But adults with Down syndrome may struggle with some tasks.

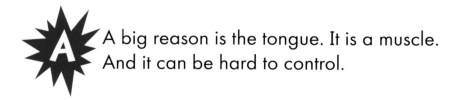

A big reason is the tongue. It is a muscle. And it can be hard to control.

Many people with Down syndrome share certain features. They have small heads and ears. They have slanted eyes. Sometimes their tongue sticks out. They are often short. And they have wide hands with short fingers. But each person with Down syndrome is different. They do not all look the same.

People with Down syndrome
are usually short. But each
person is different.

Some people have curly hair. Some people have straight hair. We look different because of chromosomes.

 How big are **chromosomes**?

What Causes Down Syndrome?

Down syndrome is not a sickness. You cannot catch it like a cold. A person is born with it. It starts inside the body's **cells**. That is where the chromosomes are. Your chromosomes determine all kinds of things about you. Are you a girl or boy? Do you have black or blond hair? Are you short or tall?

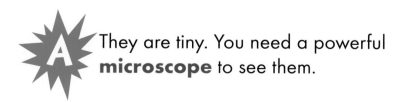

They are tiny. You need a powerful **microscope** to see them.

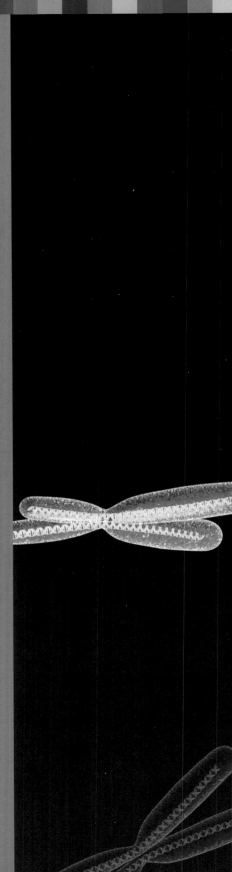

Most people have 46 chromosomes in each cell. Half of them come from your mom. The other half comes from your dad. But some people are born with 47 instead of 46. That extra chromosome causes Down syndrome.

Chromosomes are tiny. This artwork shows them large so you can see them.

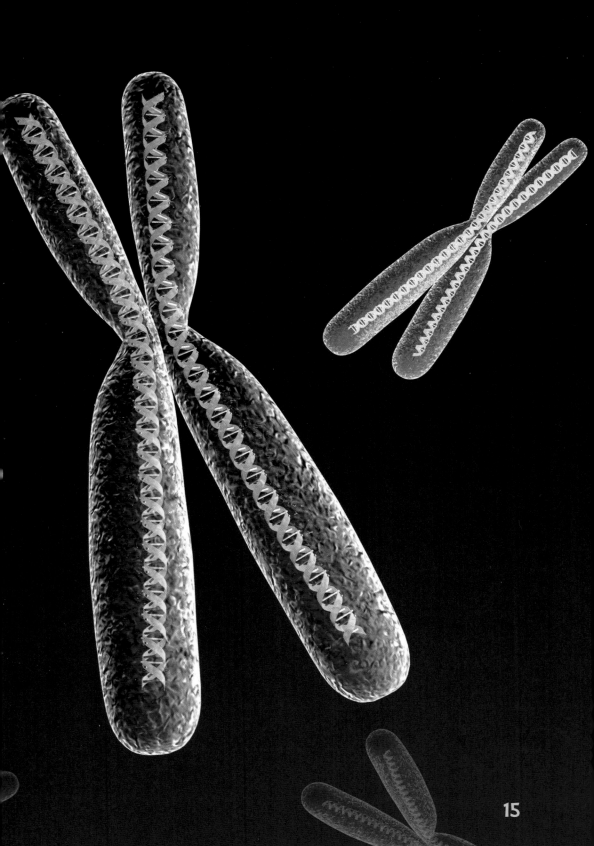

This man just finished a race. It is part of the Special Olympics.

16

Types of Down Syndrome

Every person with Down syndrome is different. They have their own personalities. They like and dislike different things. They have their own interests. They also have different levels of Down syndrome. For some people, it is severe. They need a lot of help. Everyday tasks are hard for them.

Many people with Down syndrome have a milder form of it. They learn more easily. They can do a lot of things on their own. They go to school. Some even go to college. They get jobs and have families.

 How did Down syndrome get its name?

**Dr. John Langdon Down
lived in the 1800s.**

 It is named after Dr. John Langdon Down.
He was the first to describe Down syndrome.

A physical therapist helps a little girl use her muscles.

Treating Down Syndrome

There is no cure for Down syndrome. But there is help. It comes from parents and health care workers and teachers. Together, they form a team. The team helps with all kinds of learning problems. They also help with body movement. And they teach kids and adults to speak more clearly.

Many people with Down syndrome have health problems. They may have weak eyesight or hearing. Heart problems are also common. So are stomach problems. Doctors can treat many of these problems. And many people with Down syndrome live long, healthy lives.

 How many Americans have Down syndrome?

Many people with Down syndrome are happy and healthy.

About 400,000 Americans have Down syndrome. About 6,000 babies are born with Down syndrome each year.

These people are in college. They are learning to ride the bus.

 Q My brother has Down syndrome. Why do some kids make fun of him?

Living with Down Syndrome

Kids with Down syndrome are a lot like you. They like to play with friends. They like to laugh and have fun. Most of them also go to school every day. Some of them go to special schools. These schools work with kids who have **disabilities**. But many kids with Down syndrome go to ordinary schools.

 Some kids make fun of those who are different. But being teased hurts. Everyone deserves to be respected.

Many grown-ups with Down syndrome lead full lives. They work in businesses or factories. They become writers, artists, or performers. They enjoy hobbies and sports. And they go out with friends.

Some adults with Down syndrome live with their families. Others live with roommates or helpers. Some get married. Others live on their own.

This man plays the violin for an outdoor event.

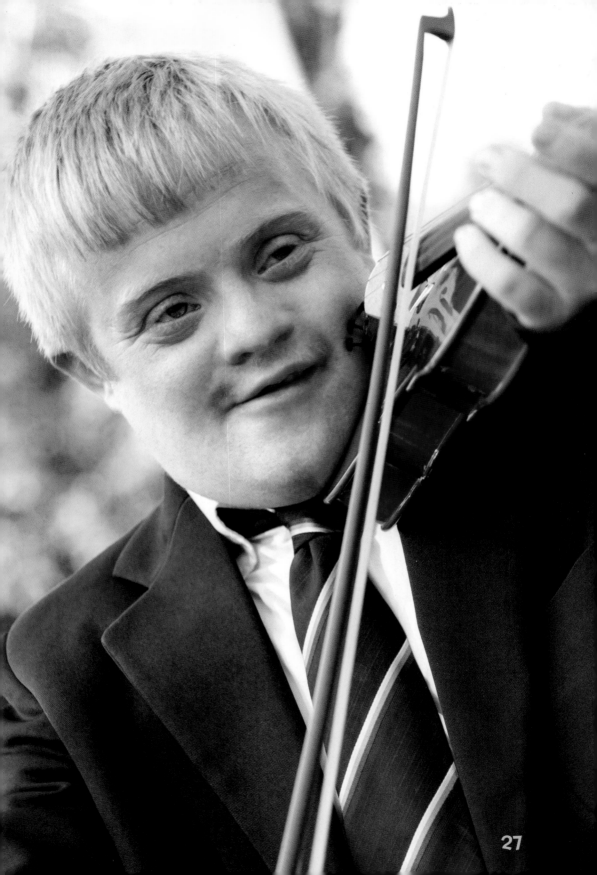

These kids have fun playing together in preschool.

Do you have a friend with Down syndrome? Find things you both like to do. Be patient when your friend speaks. Take the time to really listen. And stand up for your friend if someone is being hurtful. Then you can both have fun!

Glossary

cell The smallest part of a living thing.

chromosome Material inside each cell that determines what a person is like. Chromosomes are passed down from a person's parents.

disability A condition, illness, or injury that makes some things hard for a person to do.

Down syndrome A medical condition caused by having an extra chromosome.

microscope A tool that makes tiny things look bigger.

Read More

Bryan, Jenny. *I Have Down Syndrome*. New York: Gareth Stevens, 2011.

Parker, Vic. *I Know Someone with Down Syndrome*. Chicago: Heinemann Library, 2011.

Royston, Angela. *Explaining Down Syndrome*. Mankato, Minn.: Smart Apple Media, 2010.

Websites

KidsHealth: Down Syndrome
kidshealth.org/kid/health_problems/birth_defect/down_syndrome.html

Videos—My Great Story—National Down Syndrome Society
www.ndss.org/My-Great-Story/Videos/

What's it Like to Have Down Syndrome? — National Geographic Kids
kids.nationalgeographic.com/kids/stories/peopleplaces/downsyndrome/

Index

About the Author

Michelle Levine has written and edited many nonfiction books for children. She loves learning about new things—like Down syndrome—and sharing what she's learned with her readers. She lives in St. Paul, Minnesota.